Living the Dream
By The Sgro Family

Cover design by David L. Sgro

Published by:
The Sgro Family
439 Westwood SC PMB #138
Fayetteville, NC 28314

Edited by Cindy Barrington and Aubrey Sgro

www.Godsroadtrip.com
www.gominstries.info
DavidLSgro@gmail.com

ISBN 978-0615558509
Printed in the United States of America

Our family at Lake Atitlán, Guatemala Summer 2010 (Lake Atitlan is considered to be one of the top ten most beautiful lakes in the world!) From left to right: Jesse 15, Sam 18, David 49, Olivia 12, Angela 44, Hope 9, Giovanni 5, Noelle 2, Natalie 10, Cole 6, Rachel 16, Liam 8, Aubrey 20, Luke 13, Gabby 15.

About our family

Imagine having thirteen children. They're not adopted or from previous marriages; they're all yours! Then imagine the oldest is eighteen years. old, and the youngest is nine months. Now imagine the father is forty-eight yrs. old, and the mother is forty-three. You have two dogs, a cat, fish, a car payment, a home, a successful business, and you live in a typical "anywhere in the USA" 1 and 1/2 story raised ranch subdivision. You shop at Lowes, Best Buy, and Home Depot. You watch TV, go to church, take vacations at the beach, take your children to the movies and to their friends house...you basically live a typical American life (except, of course, the part with 13 children which is not typical anywhere). You went on a couple of week-long short term mission trips to Guatemala, and for a while, you dreamed of being a missionary; you even prayed to the Lord if it was His will, you would move wherever, whenever He said....but that was a while ago.

Those dreams came, and went. You thought those dreams died, but they didn't. One day, Thursday, 16 July 2009 at 8:20 A.M. (to be exact), the Lord called you and your spouse (separately, yet on the same day) to move to Guatemala as missionaries.

Imagine your life as if it were a snow globe, and imagine that the Lord had just picked it up, shook it and placed it back down. And then you looked at your spouse as you both realized you had just been called into full-time ministry.

At 48 and 43 yrs. old you were going to sell everything and, with your thirteen children, move to a third-world country where you knew no one; didn't speak their language; didn't know their customs; had no idea of their culture; and in fact, one of you had never been there and the other had only been there for a total of 21 days.

This is exactly what happened to David and Angela Sgro and their 13 children! This book tells their story of how they went from a family that owned a karate school and lived in the suburbs of Fayetteville, NC to selling everything and moving to Guatemala City (Mixco), which is the ninth most dangerous city in the world. Bagdad, Iraq was listed at number eight. (http://www.mediadump.com/hosted-id73-worlds-ten-most-dangerous-cities.html)

About "Living the Dream"

On Thu 16 July 2009 at 8:20am (to be exact) Angela and David clearly knew the Lord Jesus Christ wanted them to move their family to Guatemala. That they knew for sure. The rest, however, was a huge step of faith. This book strives to share the emotions, details, fears, hopes, successes, and failures of their first year.

They were robbed, dealt with trips to the doctor, had parasites, got lost, led mission trips, dealt with culture shock (to the point of a mild depression), helped feed thousands of people, took trips to Mexico to renew their visas every ninety days, and at times wondered if they lost their minds (just joking, but maybe not!) and basically got "Baptized by Fire" (Doing something "the hard way" for the first time, and being insufficiently prepared for the experience).

They experienced embarrassing faux pas (a violation of accepted social norms) and grew close as a family. They also grew in the understanding of their calling and why the Lord uprooted their family and replanted them to work amongst the extremely poor indigenous Mayans.

This book was a collaborative effort, written for our many friends and supporters. The entire family contributed to the questions and answers. You will get many different perspectives from children, teens, and adults alike. As this is a family project, no effort was put into identifying (or not identifying) who the particular writer was. Consider it part of the fun of being in a big family!

Often, when everyone is in the living-room, there is quite a bit of confusion as three or four different conversations are going on simultaneously. You might get a taste of this. Also remember the book was written over a period of about six months, so it is not in chronological order, meaning the answer to one question in the latter part of the book may say, "We are planning on doing "X" (in the future) and in the answer to another answer in an earlier portion of the book we talk about the event in the past tense because we've already started the project.

You've heard of Reality TV, well, this is a Reality Book! (Thanks Cindy!) So, WARNING, there may be parts of this book that have no rhyme or reason. Proceed reading it AT YOUR OWN RISK! And, if one day you find yourself having three or four more children than you ever imagined, or you wake up living a life of risk, fun, and adventure that you never thought possible as a missionary in some remote corner of the earth, don't blame us!

About our website:

This book is a work in progress! It is not finished. We have a website (www.Godsroadtrip.com) which can be used to augment this book. Many of the questions have a corresponding page on the website with pictures, videos, and future updates. So, sign up for the newsletter and get periodic updates and news about the release of our second book, "The day the Americans came to town", which talks about us moving into Santo Domingo Xenacoj and living amongst the Indigenous Mayas. This book is due out in early 2012.

Also, feel free to e-mail any question you have about this book, (davidlsgro@gmail.com) and I'll strive to answer your question via e-mail or in our next book.

Love, the Sgro family
www.Godsroadtrip.com
www.gominstries.info

Table of Contents:

The most commonly asked questions:

23.   How do they celebrate the holidays?

24.   What type of fruits and vegetables do they have?

25.   How do you stay in touch with your friends?

26.   What were the biggest changes for you?

27.   Do kids really sell stuff on the road alone?

28.   What is a fruit market?

29.   How do you renew your visas?

30.   What was culture shock like?

31.   What is an example of a cultural difference that caused problems?

32.   Do they have American T.V. shows?

33.   How is church different?

34.   What are schools like?

35.   What are the houses like: poor, middle class, and rich?

36.   Do they have malls?

37.   Where do you go to school?

38.   What do they wear there?

39.   Are the people friendly?

40.   What is the medical care like?

41.   Do they have heat and A/C?

42.   Do the houses have electricity?

43.   Do the houses have indoor bathrooms?

44.   Do they have hot running water?

45.   Can you drink the water?

46.   Are there hotels, and what are they like?

47. What are the most pressing issues you have noticed for women and girls?
48. How do you do school being so busy?
49. What has been the nicest experience you've gone through?
50. Do you call Guatemala "home"?
51. Will your children marry Guatemalans?
52. What do you do for a doctor?
53. What is the saddest situation you've encountered?
54. Why do you home-school, and how long have you home-schooled?
55. Is it hard having a big family?
56. Would you adopt Guatemalan children?
57. Do you have pets in Guatemala?
58. Have you met other missionaries in Guatemala?
59. What is your favorite place in Guatemala?
60. What is your weekly schedule like?
61. Are the oldest kids planning on staying in Guatemala (Rachel, Gabby, and Jesse)?
62. Is the whole family in Guatemala involved in mission work?
63. How do you live; how do you pay your bills; how do you make money?
64. How does martial arts fit into your present and future?
65. What are your plans for the future?

66. What are the difficulties in reaching a people who are so poor and have a different culture, language, and religion?

67. What is the foundation of your work there?

68. Do you ever feel discouraged or disappointed in events that occur?

69. In living by faith, how have you seen God's faithfulness show up in incredible ways?

70. Does each of you have a Bible verse that speaks to you personally?

71. Does each of you have a personality in the Bible that you relate to?

72. Are you guys willing to have more kids of your own?

73. What role has prayer played in the decisions that you have made?

74. How has living in Guatemala changed your family dynamic?

75. Where do you buy clothes?

76. What has been an impactful miracle that the Lord has done?

77. Do you work with a church in Guatemala?

78. What spiritual warfare have you encountered?

79. Have any of you gotten sick down there?

80. What are the main problems that you see in Guatemala?

81. How do you know you stand out in Guatemala?

82. How often do you come back to the US?

83. Is there a final story you'd like to share?

84. How can we help you, your family, and your ministry?

85. What are you plans for the next "Chapter" or next year couple of years?

The most commonly asked questions:

1. What is Guatemala like, and do you like it?

Guatemala is a very beautiful but very poor country. There are mountains and volcanoes everywhere you look. Trees and flowers grow abundantly due to the climate. Although it is a very beautiful country, the streets are cluttered with garbage as most people do not have regular garbage pickup, and they don't think twice about throwing their garbage on the street. There are slums and very poor housing everywhere you go.

Guatemala has many dirt, country roads where you will often see people walking their cows or horses loaded down with wood for sale. It is very common to see chickens and roosters wandering around the roads. Most people walk as they cannot afford cars here, so it is common to see whole families walking and laughing together. The Guatemalan people are very happy despite their poor living conditions.

You will see mothers with babies tied to their backs and small dirty children around their feet working in the fields, or selling various items along the road. Women walk with baskets of freshly made tortillas for sale. The Guatemalan people are hard workers. They work from early morning until late at night. The whole family usually works together. It is a common sight to see children along with their parents picking up pieces of wood on the road that they will either sell or use to cook their dinner over.

There are also busy, city streets where you will see children as young as five years old selling gum, candy, toys, flowers, and newspapers, all alone at all times of the day. We often see kids dressed as clowns and performing juggling tricks or men blowing fire for a few coins. Old men and women, who should be home drinking coffee and reading the newspaper, are seen begging on the streets for money. Young mothers with their children all around them beg on streets that are so busy you would never want to drive on, never mind beg with your small children next to you.

The busy roads are lines with people selling fruit, vegetables, water, soda, and chips to anyone that will slow down. They get your attention by yelling or standing in the street or coming right up to your car trying to sell you something. If your window is closed and tinted, as ours are, they will often tap on the window to get your attention.

It can be a little overwhelming as you see and hear things that you would never see in the US. We have grown quite accustomed to these sights after our time here. But we are constantly amazed by some of the things we see. For instance, a man leading six or more goats down a busy city street is different, or men without legs riding around on skateboards begging on the side of the road; this is not something we've seen in the US.

2.   Why Guatemala?

Dave is often asked, "Why Guatemala?" In 1999, we moved from Groton, CT to Fayetteville, NC. When we first moved to Fayetteville, Dave took a job as a carpenter. As his job placed him with men who were from Mexico (and looking back, he's sure there were people from Guatemala), he was led to start praying for Mexico and Central America. In 2002, a student joined his karate school and told him about his work in Guatemala. It sounded like fun, and in 2004, he (with Aubrey, Sam, and Rachel, who were thirteen, twelve, and nine years old at the time) visited for the first time and the rest is history!

Guatemala is really beautiful, and once we moved here, we began to see such a diverse country. There are 23 different languages. There are 18 different climate zones. Guatemala is very diverse!

3.   Do you speak Spanish?

NO! Once we realized the Lord had called us to move to Guatemala, Dave started visiting on a regular basis. While none of us spoke Spanish, we quickly found ourselves studying and gaining as much Spanish as we could. Since we moved to Guatemala we've all taken some schooling. We had a teacher coming to our house for about the first six months.

In March 2011, we moved to Santo Domingo Xenacoj, Sac which is about 30 minutes from Antigua which has 70 Spanish schools. All in all between studying in school, using Spanish on a daily basis, and having our friends help us and correct us, we're all beginning to see our Spanish improve! BUT, we still have a long way to go! Of course, the children are learning so much faster than their parents! It drives us crazy when we have to ask our children to translate for us. However, we are very proud of them and how fast they have adapted and learned how to live in Guatemala!

4. Do you like Guatemala better than the States?

There are some things about Guatemala that we really, really like. The fruits and vegetables are very, very fresh, and inexpensive. The people are really friendly. The climate is almost perfect at 6,300 - 7,000 ft above sea level (55 - 75 degrees year round).

Also, above all else, we know we are supposed to be here, so having a calling from God gives you a love for the land, the people, the culture, and your life there in general. We wouldn't say we like living in Guatemala better, because living in the U.S. is like a dream come true. Life is amazing living in the United States, because there is so much and so much to do.

However, we see the poverty and the great need, and realize that God has directed us here with the understanding that this is where we are supposed to be at this time in our lives. Because of that, we enjoy life here.

5.   What do you miss about the US?

This list could really go on forever!   Of course, first and foremost, we miss Aubrey and Sam (our two eldest children living in North Carolina). We really miss them, and we know they miss us, too.

We also miss our church, Manna Church of Fayetteville! We miss listening to Pastor Michael Fletcher on Sunday mornings. Yes, he has an online broadcast, and we really appreciate it, but there is nothing like sitting in a service together with hundreds of other believers! Manna Church is more than a place we attended on Sundays; the community there is our extended family. Manna is still a big part of our lives, but we miss going on a regular basis and being a part of a such a big community of believers.

Twizzlers' candy is another thing people in the U.S. take for granted! Or, for example, the ability to buy peanut butter that doesn't cost $8 a jar. Angie really likes butter, but our butter here is imported from New Zealand, and tastes very different than what we're used to. Every time I (David) go back to the U.S., I bring some butter home for Angie, and that makes her happy.

6. How did you (the thirteen children) feel when your parents told you about moving?

We were excited, but didn't know what to think. We never thought we would move to Guatemala before they told us. We had a bunch of questions, like: when are we moving, what is it like there, what are we going to do there, are we ever coming back?

When Giovanni, who was four years old at the time, heard, he ran in the corner and cried and said, "I am not going." Everyone else was cheering and happy but here our four year old was very upset. When we asked him why he was so upset, he said, "I do not have a bed there, and what about my toys, and clothes, and my sucky blanket?" When we reassured him that we would get him a bed, and he could bring his clothes, toys, and sucky blanket, he was much happier. So the next morning, he came down with his backpack full of stuff, and said, "Okay Mom I am ready; let's go." The older kids (teens) were not quite as excited because they realized they would have to leave all their friends and everything they knew.

There was so much to do to prepare for the move, and the kids had to go through everything they owned and only keep their very favorite things. That was sometimes difficult, but really they were so good about it. We were so proud of them. Everyone only had two suitcases full of stuff that they could take, so we either got rid of everything else or stored it.

We lived in Fayetteville for ten years, and we have thirteen kids, so you can just imagine how much stuff we had to get rid of. We had numerous yard sales, and after a while, we just began to give stuff away.

The smaller kids went through all their toys and just kept their very favorite ones, and Dave brought them to Guatemala early so when we got here they would be here for them. However, when we arrived we soon found out that all their precious toys and books had been stolen. Our house was robbed and all of the children's favorite toys were gone.

That was our welcoming to Guatemala. We arrived and opened the doors and the kids ran to check out their new house and saying how it was going to be like Christmas because they were going to get to play with all their favorite toys again, but they were gone. We were robbed. We had to rent two condos, side by side because of the size of our family, so we think the workers who opened the wall took the toys. Of course, Dave confronted the manager of the condo, and of course, he knew nothing, not even contact information for the workers. Welcome to Guatemala!

Anyway, regarding all the mission toys...well, we had some pretty sad children, so Dave said, "Who wants to take a ride and get some NEW TOYS?" The children were excited but it was very hard for me, Angela, because some of those books I had since my oldest (who is now twenty-one) was a little girl. Copies of those books could be re-bought, but they originals could never be replaced.

At first when we, as a family, realized we were called to Guatemala, it was difficult on our older three children. Aubrey was working as a R.U.S.H. (Reaching Unreached Student Harvest) campus minister at the time. RUSH is a program that starts Bible studies at schools and provides Biblical guidance for the challenges of the teen years.

Aubrey, while excited that her family was called to serve as full time missionaries in Guatemala, also enjoyed working with RUSH. We, the parents, really wanted Aubrey in Guatemala, but as time passed and we started to see what her life would look like in Guatemala, we came to the realization that it would be better for her to stay in Fayetteville.

In Guatemala we were going to be living in Guatemala City (Mixco), which was dangerous. In Fayetteville, Aubrey had a car, friends, and a purpose. She had a degree of freedom. She could just hop in the car and meet friends for lunch at Red Robin. She had just finished her college degree and was working her first full time job. If she moved to Guatemala, what would she do? We only had one vehicle, a fifteen passenger van, so she wasn't going to have the same freedoms. She would not be able to drive wherever and whenever she wanted. She wouldn't have a job which meant she would have little to no income. Her life and activities would be severely curtailed.

It was a sad day as we realized that Aubrey would not be moving with us. Usually the college graduate leaves the nest, but we pulled the nest out from under her. I have to admit, I, David, felt guilt and sadness about this. While I knew we, Angela and I, were clear about our calling from the Lord, I also was coming to terms with some of the ramifications of our huge decision. So as we came to the decision that Aubrey would not be moving to Guatemala, while we felt peace about the decision, we, as a family, began to feel the weight of this decision. We started to see, for the first time, that our family would not be living together.

And then it began to occur to me, if Aubrey wasn't going to move with us, what about Sam? Sam was eighteen year old, and what would Sam do in Guatemala? While Sam wasn't as established as Aubrey, he was beginning to stand on his own. For the first six months, Sam lived in neither Guatemala nor the U.S., and he lived in both Guatemala and the U.S. In other words, he lived in limbo. He wasn't sure.

I suppose someone might have said, "Well, you should have waited until all the children were grown up before you moved to the mission field." Noelle being only 9 months old when the Lord called us to the mission field; had we waited until she was on her own, we would have been in our late 60's early 70's. So, we knew that by leaving Fayetteville one of the children would be caught between "here" (wherever "here" was) and "there" (wherever "there" was).

It was Sam. For the first eight months he'd come to Guatemala for a couple of months and then back to the U.S. for a couple of months. Angela and I wanted to let some time pass because we knew Sam was figuring it out. After about 6 months, Sam, Angie and I knew it would be best for Sam to choose one or the other. It was difficult for him to be in both places because he couldn't build anything. He couldn't get a job in the U.S. because in two or three months he'd be coming back to Guatemala.

So after about 8 months of back and forth, Sam decided to call the U.S. "home". That meant after his March 2011, visit Sam would be returning to the U.S. to live. Even though I knew it was best for him, it was hard for Angie and me. Sam is a great kid. He is easy going. Angela loves to hear him play the piano. Sam is funny, and we just love him and having him home, but we wanted what was best for him. Having him travel back and forth between Guatemala and the U.S.A. wasn't best for him, and so we had to say goodbye to our second child.

Rachel had started college early, so did Aubrey. Because we home schooled and because both Rachel and Aubrey are school-minded and incredibly smart, they both started college early. They both attended Grace College of Divinity which was located on the Manna Church Campus in Fayetteville. At 16 Rachel was in her second semester of college (I *think* it was her 2nd semester), whatever it was, she had already completed some classes so she knew what college was like.   She really wanted to stay in Fayetteville for her schooling and suggested she stay with some friends, the Choi's. Again, Angie and I were really torn. Could we leave our 16 yr. old with another family? Could we move to Guatemala without Rachel? Was leaving your minor child with another family responsible? Was leaving your minor child with another family irresponsible?

This was really a difficult decision. Rachel felt like she could handle it, and Aubrey was going to be here too. Aubrey and Rachel had a close friendship, and with us moving to Guatemala, I knew they would be even closer. Also, knowing how much Rachel wanted to stay in the U.S., Angela and I discussed it and weighed both options.

In the end we decided to let her stay. We felt if we forced her to move to Guatemala, she would resent it. She would come because she "had to" and in the end would only dream of moving back to the U.S., and as soon as she turned eighteen years. old, we were concerned she would run back to the U.S., and we didn't want this. We didn't want her to resent being in Guatemala. So we decided she needed to follow her desire for college.

She came down to Guatemala for our first summer, and in August 2010, she returned home with Aubrey for her new life in Fayetteville living with her friends. Allowing our sixteen year old daughter to move back to the U.S. and live without us was a very, very difficult decision. There were some very real difficult ramifications of following God at all cost. There were some immediate heart-breaking (unseen) realities in our decision in becoming Missionaries.

We never, not for one second, ever felt we had made a mistake. We have never regretted our decision to become Missionaries. Yes, there are days it can be tough, real tough, but what person doesn't face tough days. Angie and I feel it is tough enough living in Gods will; we simply couldn't imagine living outside of His will.

What would our life have been like if we clearly knew God wanted us to be in Guatemala, and we ignored Him? We simply couldn't imagine what life would be like without His favor. We feel to live outside of Gods clear will is wrong. It's a rebellion, and that was not what we wanted for ourselves. Honestly, once we clearly knew God called us, we knew we were going and never doubted what we were doing, where we were going, or why. We put our hand to the plow and never looked back.

But that doesn't mean it will be easy. We were coming to terms with the fact that our three oldest children would not be with us, and the reality of living in Guatemala with three of our children back in the U.S. was really hard to deal with. We were going through a very tough period. We ended up living in Guatemala City, which was much more expensive than planned; our original budget was based on living near Antigua, but plans were shifted three months before we moved. So after being in country for three or four months, we realized I was going to have to return to the U.S. for some fundraising.

This was a really difficult time for Angela. Life was very different for her, and it got very difficult, real quick. I had to start heading back to the U.S. to fundraise. It was "back to school time," so Aubrey and Rachel were gone now.

When we lived in the U.S., we owned a karate school and sub-rented some of our space to a dance school. So the children's karate and dance classes were in the same location. So at around 4 P.M., four days a week, like a school bus, Angie would drive the children to the karate school. They would pile out of the van and pile into the karate school. Then they'd peel off to their respective class. Around 6 P.M., the van would drive in front of the karate school and the kids would pile back in. Then Angela would drive home; feed the kids some dinner, and that was her routine.

But in Guatemala she didn't have this routine. She couldn't drive because it was too dangerous for her to drive in Guatemala. We didn't have a karate school any more. We didn't really know anyone. We really didn't have any friends. We thought we'd have lots of friends because we joined a large church as missionaries, but the reality is that this simply wasn't happening. We were really beginning to feel alone, and it was a difficult time. I would even go as so far as to say we suffered some mild depression, a "cabin fever" if you will.

But we worked through it, came through the culture shock wall, and caught our second wind! God did it. He never left us and His Holy Spirit encouraged us. He always knew exactly what we needed and when. As I learned more and more about the City, I'd discover an American restaurant, or we'd take trip to Antigua, or something would pop up. We made it and we know God is good! Taste and see that the Lord is good! I hope this book motivates you to endure, as God is good!

7. What do you do there?

As missionaries, we serve our home church, Manna Church, in the mission field. We love how Manna Church is a mission oriented Church. We host about seven or eight short term mission teams coming to Guatemala. These teams come from many different Churches and denominations. Our teams are relational based, as opposed to denominational based. If you want to serve the poor to fulfill the Bibles mandate to "GO!" then this is a ministry for you!

It takes a lot of prep work for several months before a team arrives. We have to visit everywhere they will sleep, eat, and work. We arrange their food, their transportation, their lodging, and translators. We arrange it all.

In June 2010, our first summer here, we hosted two teams. On the first trip we hosted a combined short term mission team from Manna Church in Fayetteville, NC and Bethel Temple Assembly of God from Hampton, VA. In many ways this trip simply was a disaster. In many ways this trip was an amazing success. It was the best of times and it was the worst of times!

This trip was the first trip I would lead and run while living in Guatemala. We were only in country for several weeks before the team arrived, and this was my first trip which would be planned and led from my new church. I had just met the church in March 2010 and was moving to Guatemala in June of 2010. On this trip I made plans with one of the pastors to visit his school district for our first mission trip in July.

I visited again for a week in April 2010. Things were falling in place. Plans were made, and in

April, we went over the plan again. Everything looked good. We would visit four schools per day for three days performing a karate demo, a drama, and an evangelistic message, just as I had done on the four previous trips in 2004, 2007, 2008 and 2009.

I visited again in May and reviewed the plans again. For three months (March, April, and May) I visited and made all the plans to visit twelve different schools in three days. I was suppose to fly down several weeks before we moved to furnish the house, but right before we moved Guatemala erupted.

There was an earthquake, a volcanic eruption, and a tropical storm which dumped 36 inches of rain in one hour. In Guatemala City, a ten story sink hole swallowed a city intersection (Google "Guatemala City Sink Hole). Hundreds of roads and bridges were destroyed. Many people died.

All this happened right before we moved there. Of course, when you know someone moving to Guatemala, your awareness of Guatemala increases, so many people started sending me stories about how violent Guatemala was. I caught a lot of flack from friends and family about taking my family to Guatemala. Everyone was calling me, asking if I was still going to move. I felt like a man who becomes a firefighter, and on his first day of work, a call comes in for a team to respond because a building is on fire.

Right before he jumps on the truck, his friend calls and says "Hey, did you hear the building is on fire?" When he responds "Yes", his friend says "Well, are you still going to the building?" The firefighter replies "Yes, I'm going now!", to which his friend says "But it's on fire, it's dangerous, are you sure you want to go?" Finally, he responds: "I'M A FIRE FIGHTER! This is what I do, this is what I was trained for, this is what I signed up for, THIS IS WHAT I LIVE FOR!"

Angie and I knew the Lord told us to go, and it is to Him alone we must answer, even if there is a cost. I had one friend who really laid into me. I knew he was just concerned about my family and I, which I appreciated, but it seemed like his criticism wasn't going to end.

So, I went online and investigated the crime near where he lived and sent him the link to several stories which included several murders in his city. I told him it was dangerous where he lived, and he should move to a safer place to live right away. He stopped bothering me about living in Guatemala.

I was supposed to fly down to Guatemala several weeks before we moved. I was going to take a week and set up the house. As it simply was too expensive to ship down the appliances, beds, and everything, we decided to move down with just two suitcases and buy everything new in Guatemala.

I had price shopped everything and the difference between shipping my old washing machine to Guatemala, and buying a new one was about $50. This was the same with everything, so we decided it would be better to simply buy new.

I was to arrive and take a week to set everything up. Angie and I never had new everything, so in many ways this was an exciting time. However, all the flights were cancelled because there was volcanic ash in the air. The week came and went, and I couldn't catch a flight to Guatemala. I would have to arrive with literally two suit cases each.

When I arrived, I found out we couldn't go directly to our new home. The excessive amount of rain caused a 150 foot section of the security wall around our condo unit to collapse. The local church we were involved with arranged for us to stay in a hotel. We arrived on a Thursday and we stayed at the hotel that night. The hotel was the Grand Tikal Futura which is a really nice hotel. There were several nice swimming pools and huge chandeliers. Olivia said "Wow, Dad, I really like living in Guatemala!" I just laughed and said to myself "Enjoy it because it wont last".

Early the next morning, I met with one of the pastors and a pick-up truck, and we went shopping for beds. It was a thirteen hour day, as we had to shop, buy, and transport bedding for our huge family. It took several days to get settled in. We had a team coming in one week, and my first set of plans were about to go up in smoke.

I met with the Evangelism pastor one last time to go over the plans we had made, and he said to me, "We can't visit schools next week; all the schools are on vacation." Are you kidding me? Are you serious? I've been planning this with you for three months, and it's just now you realized the schools are on vacation next week???

Actually, I wanted to say all these things, but I couldn't bring myself to do it. I just smiled and said. "Okay." This was my first very hard, very real experience of culture shock. I had my first mission team coming in about a week. I had nothing in my house except beds, and I was in panic mode. I decided I'd call some orphanages, but found that they were all booked at least year in advance! So, plan number two went up in smoke. What was I going to do?

I prayed for a while. I met with one of the pastors of the church and felt that with all the natural disasters, there must be someone somewhere who needs help. He said the families around the volcano that erupted were in bad shape. So the next day, my family and I took a ride to the area around the volcano; there is some good video footage on our website about this. After seeing the devastation and the need, we decided we would take our team there.

We made food and housing arrangements. In making arrangements for the team to arrive, I was able to line up a pastor who had a truck, and I had rented a van. I told the pastor we would need another van to transport the team, but he insisted it would be fine. I knew it wouldn't be, so I told him again that we needed another van, and again he said it would be fine. I was running into another cultural wall. I took a breath and said, "I really think we need another van," and he said, "Don't worry; it will be fine".

At this point, I had to make a decision. My team was a group of my friends. They would be here for a week and would leave. However, this pastor lived here and was the person I was going to have to work with for who knows how long. The team was going to have to take the hit.

Sure enough, the team arrived and when the pastor looked at how many people there were and how big they were (the average Americans are much bigger than the people in Guatemala, and I had several big karate guys on the team, too), and how much luggage they had, he looked at me and neither of us said a word, but you know I wanted to say something.

At that point, I knew had a problem. I knew it beforehand and did all I could to try to resolve it. I just looked at the pastor and we got everyone in the van and truck. I know my folks were stuffed in like sardines, and I knew it wasn't a great start to the trip. We were supposed to head straight to the volcano, but we still had to buy supplies. I frantically found a place for us to stay that night, so we headed over to the facility where we would be staying.

The food supplies for two hundred families were supposed to arrive by 10 A.M. the next morning. Several hours later, food for seventy-five families arrived, but only forty bags. The team quickly assembled the bags, and then there was nothing to do but wait. The hours ticked by. Finally, in the afternoon, the other supplies arrived.

The road to the volcano was treacherous to drive. We were supposed to make two trips with the food, but at the last minute, the two days were combined into one. Welcome to another cultural shock! In Guatemala plans can change on a moment's notice. We Americans want everything planned, down to the last detail, in advance. But in Guatemala, everything is fluid. This was very obvious and frustrating, because every plan I made was falling apart in front of my eyes, and my team was also beginning to see this.

We loaded up everything for the entire 200 families (12,000 lbs. of food in a 6,000 lb truck) and headed to the volcano. On the way there, we learned the road had been shut down, but we continued anyway. We got to our first of two destinations, and it started to rain and rain and rain. The pastor said that we had to move quickly because the road down the volcano would become very dangerous, so we passed out the food supplies as quickly as possible.

There's an old saying, "All's well that ends well," but this mission trip was a rough "first one out the chute". We learned a lot, especially about cultural differences and being flexible. We quickly improved, as we had another team coming right away.

Our second team built outdoor bathrooms for a local kids' club that feeds 120 poor children on a daily basis. They also did street evangelism, helped feed the kids every morning, and performed a drama at a local church. Things went much smoother with this team.

In August 2010, we brought food, medicine, clothing, toys, and a new concrete stove, to a family of seventeen, seven of which were adopted. All seventeen people were living in two bedrooms, so we built a third bedroom for them. We bought new beds and the bedding for them.

In October 2010, we had a Harvest Fest for some very poor children that live at 6,500 square feet above sea level. They live in lamina (tin) houses, where it can get into the forties at night. We had games, face painting, and 10 piñatas for them. Best of all, we were able to give each child a warm blanket to help them sleep more comfortably.

In December 2010, we brought Christmas presents to 1,250 kids, who would otherwise not have any presents at all. We went to an orphanage, a dump, the previously mentioned kids' club, and many very poor villages. This trip really broke our hearts, as the reality of where we lived and what we were doing was starting to seep in.

In serving the poor, there is great satisfaction, but also great heartache. Jesus Christ was a man acquainted with grief and sorrows, and I was learning this as a missionary. I found myself praying and crying much more than I had in the past. We were all praying more, and our hearts were breaking more and more.

In February 2011, we relocated from the large city of Mixco to the much smaller area of Sumpango, which was about forty minutes further into the mountains. We began work on building a chicken coop for our feeding program. Angie has always wanted chickens, and this was finally her chance. We planned on starting out with fifty chickens.

In March 2011, we had another short term mission team come for a week. The group is named "The Experience," which is a one-year intensive internship program at Grace College of Divinity in Fayetteville, NC. This program is designed to solidify and build their Christian foundation before they go to college.

The Experience team did street evangelism, visited a local university, and elementary school. The team saw thirty-five people accept the Lord, which included two teens, (fifteen and sixteen year olds) who had admittedly committed many murders as gang members. These teens said that The Experience loved and accepted them without judging them, which led them to leave their gang lives. They admitted many of their friends had already been killed, and their decision to leave the gang could also result in their death. However, they didn't care, because they wanted to leave that lifestyle.

The following week, we hosted a medical mission trip and brought medical attention and medicine to eight hundred people. This was very rewarding and sad at the same time. It was easy to see our team was really helping people, but at the same time, we knew there were many more that needed help, and seeing the living conditions of these people was breaking our hearts.

We were beginning to feel we needed to find an area and dig deep. We had hosted six short term mission teams by now, and Angie wanted a place of her own. Pastor Michael Fletcher, Senior Pastor of our Manna, our home church, went to the mayor of Fayetteville, NC and asked which area needed the most help. The answer was a government housing project called Campbell Terrace. So, Manna Church adopted Campbell Terrace. This meant bringing clothing, Christmas presents, block parties, Bible studies, friendship and support.

Angela told me she wanted her own "Campbell Terrace" here in Guatemala. In Guatemala, we had been doing a lot of great things, but it was difficult to plan trips in which we were doing ministry in areas four or five hours way. There was so much involved. First, I needed to find an area and meet with the local contact. Then, I'd need to set up housing, food, work details, security, and translators (with twenty different Mayan Languages, not dialects- but ACTUAL different languages). It was very difficult to find competent translators. One challenge was actually finding and contacting them.

The next challenge was dealing with them not showing up, or showing up one day but not the next.

Ultimately, we had so many moving pieces, that we had to simplify our short term mission trips. The planning for the teams were consuming a lot of time and resources. We asked God to lead us to an area where we could set up shop. We would focus the majority of our teams to one area, and at the time of writing this book we were focusing on a town known as "Santo Domingo Xenacoj", or simply "Xenacoj" (pronounced "Shen" "Ah" "Kowe." The "owe" part of "Kowe" is pronounced just like it is spelled, like "I owe you a cup of coffee!"). "Xenacoj" means "Under the roar of the lion". I was told this may had been because when the village was first founded the villagers may have heard the mountain lions in the woods.

Since moving to Xenacoj in February 2011, we really have done a lot. We opened a church. We offer karate, dance, and English classes all for free. On Saturday mornings, we scramble up 120 to 150 eggs, and serve black beans and tortillas to 120 -150 poor people. That is a lot of work. We have the elderly, teens, and children coming every week. Some of them are so hungry that they have three or four helpings. Some of them ask for a plate to bring some home for them later, and we all know how awful leftover eggs are. We've seen old ladies putting extra eggs in their purses to bring home with them. After breakfast we have karate, and dance classes and then show a movie in Spanish to the kids. We always serve drinks and cookies with the movie. Also, the kids and Angela are teaching English at a public school once a week.

8.　　How long are you going to live there?

Now that is a good question! People often ask us this question, and we tell them we will live here until God tells us to move somewhere else. Right now it looks like we will be here for a very long time, but only God knows how long that is. We will live here until God says otherwise. In other words, we bought one-way tickets here and currently have no plans to move back. We will visit the U.S. from time to time because we do miss our friends and family, but Guatemala is our home.

9.　　Do you have any friends?

Yes, we have friends. It is pretty easy for the kids to make friends, even with the language barrier. Since we have moved out of the city to Xenacoj, and have opened up our own space, we have met many people. They play every time we go there, and still manage to communicate even though they speak very little English. It doesn't seem to matter at all to them. We have only known them for about three months but they feel like we have known them much longer.

10.   How difficult is the language barrier?

The language barrier is super difficult and very frustrating. A simple thing like going to the store and wanting to buy confectionary sugar is so hard when you do not know how to say it in Spanish. If you have to go to the doctor for something and cannot explain what is wrong, it can be so hard. It was especially hard the first year. It is still difficult, but we know a little more Spanish now, we also know some people who can help translate for us. We do not know enough Spanish to fully explain ourselves, and that is very frustrating.

I, David, found this very tough at first. I had to buy everything. When we moved here we only had two suitcases each, so we had to replace everything: bedding, major appliances (washer, dryer, refrigerator, freezer, stove), then all the minor appliances (microwave, coffee maker, toaster, blender, pancake grill,) then plates, pots, pans, silverware, tables, cooking utensils, and then in the living room: T.V., sofa, chairs, and on and on. I had to do this with a very limited understanding of Spanish!   Fortunately for us the church we were working with assigned some people to help us. But still, they could not always be there, and after a while we were on our own.

11.   How is the food different?

Well, for one thing everyone loves tortillas here. Every place you go you will see ladies making hundreds of them daily. And they eat black beans or rice on everything. Some of my kids really love tortillas, black beans, and rice. Every traditional restaurant you go to will serve tortillas, black beans, and rice. They use a lot more sauces on their foods then in the U.S. They smother their meat in sauce. They love cake, but they love cake that has fruit in or on it. When I want cake, I want good old fashioned chocolate cake. But, if you offered a Guatemalan any cake in the store they would choose cake with fruit.

I pretty much cook all American food here in the house, though we have learned to make tortillas. The milk and cheese, butter, and ice cream is NOT as good as in the U.S. We really miss those items a lot. We buy a lot of imported food because some of the food just does not taste good. Pancake syrup for instance, is so watery, and the kids do not like it, so we buy American brands. We try to buy Guatemalan brands when we can because it is cheaper, but some things we just do not like.

As we live here longer and longer we are slowly discovering more items they simply don't have here. We're also discovering new stores that have exactly what we want. When Dave goes back to the States he brings back a couple of suitcases with stuff from the US that we can't get here. We love it!

12.   How are the stores different?

They have Wal-Mart here, but it is different. I miss Wal-Mart in the U.S. I never thought I would say that, but I do. I miss being able to walk into a store and buy whatever I want. Many of the stores simply don't have much of the items from the U.S. On every isle there are three or four people standing there with an item they are trying to sell, and wanting to help you. It is like that in any store you go in here people follow you around wanting to help. Sometimes it's nice, but sometimes it's just plain annoying. I always say for such a poor country there are more shoe stores then I have ever seen in my life!

It's also incredible that for such a poor country that there are few stores available for rent, everything seems rented. They have tons of little stores that sell everything you could think of. The malls are huge and expensive. One mall has a roller coaster inside of it and a Ferris wheel outside of it, and many of the smaller malls have play areas for children with slides and swings. Sometimes I just wish I could drive to Target or Kohl's or a REAL Wal-Mart where I know where everything is and they have just what I want.

13.   What is the driving like?

In the city, it is crazy. They don't use lanes or blinkers. I never drive in the city, only Dave drives in the city. Also, it can be dangerous if you make a wrong turn; you can't really ask for directions; it could be dangerous. In Xenacoj where we work, it is just a quiet village, so the driving is better. But it is very difficult driving on those narrow streets with a big old 15 passenger van. Public transportation is how a lot of people get around here. They crowd way too many people into the buses and drive very fast. They load all their stuff on top of the buses; it is quite a sight.

You will often see four people on a motorcycle that includes: a dad, small child, mom, and very small baby. Crazy! They drive with kids on their laps, and people crowded into the back of pickups, and, really, you have to see it to believe it. We've seen motorcycles with an expandable ladder tied to some poles that ride over head on motorcycles. We've seen 60 pound propane tanks strapped to the back seat of a motorcycle; now that is dangerous. We've seen things that just make us wonder and scratch our heads. We've seen four people standing up in the sliding doorway of a van, which is allowed, but I've been told I can't walk into a Wal-Mart with a McDonald's coffee, go figure?!?

14. What was it like to sell everything?

In some ways it wasn't hard at all. Most Americans have way too much stuff, and a family of fifteen has even more than most. We had an attic that was full of all kinds of stuff, so we went through everything which was a big job, let me tell you. Then we said, "What do we really need. What can we live without, and what do we want to put in storage?"

The kids were so good about it. They went through all their toys and just kept their very favorite things. Before we moved here, Dave brought all their toys to our condo, so when we got here, it would already be here, but it was all stolen. That was very difficult. It was all their favorite toys and books that we had since my oldest daughter was little.

15. Did you keep anything; what was it?

Yes, we kept some of our favorite things. The kids kept their toys and books. We kept some items that could not be replaced, like our table, hutch, china dishes, Christmas decorations that we have had forever, photo albums, baby books, etc. We put all that in storage in the U.S. and hope to get it here someday.   Each time Dave goes to Fayetteville he tries to bring back a little bit of our stuff.

16.   What happened to your animals in the U.S.?

We had two dogs and a cat. Dave found a home for our cat quite quickly, but finding a home for our two slightly older dogs was a challenge (Mico and Panther).   Dave decided to post on Facebook to my friends that I had two dogs ages eight and seven. Very quickly we had a response! A friend's mother from Connecticut had recently lost her dog, so she was quite excited when she heard there were two elderly dogs that needed a home.   We were told the dogs would be spoiled! They would be eating the soft canned dog food (we served dry dog food); they would be sleeping in the bed at night with their new owners (they we outside dogs with us and only came inside during extreme heat or extremely cold days).

Dave visited CT in the fall of 2010 and saw them about 4 months after we gave them away. They looked great. He could see they were really loved and even had put on some weight.   Honestly, they are much better off, and God really gave these guys "the bomb" when it comes to doggy retirement!

17.   What was it like traveling with the whole family?

Well, it was quite an adventure. Traveling to Guatemala took a total of three days. First we had to drive to Florida which we broke up into two days because driving to Miami with everyone can be a bit stressful. After two days of driving we finally arrived to Miami. The next morning was our flight to Guatemala. When the shuttle bus arrived the next morning, we packed it with all our bags and headed out to the airport. Once we got there, I could tell God was really with us because there were a few people working at the airport that came and brought us to the front of the line.

We were checked in with our plane tickets in fifteen minutes. When we were going through customs, one of the guys working there came up to Angela and asked her if we had a camera crew with us, and that we should have a show. We had a lot of comments like that.   Then finally, we were off to Guatemala, the beginning of our new lives! When we looked into buying one-way tickets for 12 people to fly from Raleigh, NC (RDU) to Guatemala City (GUA) the flights cost about $650. By God's grace.

I discovered Spirit Air, and a one-way flight from Ft Lauderdale, FL (FLL) was only $200. To fly with 2 checked bags, it was about $50 more.   So by flying out of FLL, we saved $400 per person or about $4,800! WE WERE FLYING OUT OF FLL! But, each bag weighed 50 lbs; so our checked luggage would be about 1,200 lbs! Plus everyone had a carry-on bag at about 35 lbs, which was 12 bags at 35 lbs, 420 lbs, and a personal bag at about 20 lbs, or 240 lbs. So our total travel weight was about 1900, close to a ton!

So on Tuesday, 15 June 2010, we pulled up our anchor and set sail for Guatemala City (Mixco), Guatemala. Angie's brother, Tony, lived near Jacksonville, FL (J'ville), so our plan was to break the 12 hr. drive into two parts. The first day (Tuesday, 15 June 2010), we would cover from Fayetteville, NC to J'ville, FL. We got a late start though and didn't pull into J'ville until late.

The next leg of the trip was J'ville to Ft Lauderdale. We had to leave early on Wednesday (16 June 2010) because once we checked into the hotel, I then had to return the U-Hall trailer and then drive to the shipping port to drop off the van. I had set up shipping the van with Crowley out of Miami. If you've never shipped a van internationally and you have to set up all the logistics, let me tell you, it is a lot of paperwork and a pain in the neck! Also, it was supposed to take two weeks to get the van. It ended up taking over 6 weeks for us to get our van, so we ended up having to rent a van for our first month in Guatemala.

18.   How is the weather?

The average temperature around 6,300 ft. above sea level ranges from the 50's to the mid 80's. No one has heat or air-conditioning in Guatemala because they don't need it, and most folks couldn't afford it anyway. We love the weather here. When it is colder, in the evenings, the temperature in our house averages around 55 degrees, so we simply use extra blankets and light a fire.

During the dry season, it is about 75-80 degrees in the day, and then during the night, it cools down, sometimes enough for a fire. Yes, it does get cold here, especially in the mountains. Since we are south of Mexico, and parts of Mexico are really, really, hot, I can understand why people would think Guatemala is very hot. Except, we live and work between 6,300 - 7,000 ft. about sea level. The average year round temperature is around 70 degrees.

We have two seasons, wet and dry. The dry season is from October to May, and the wet season is from May to October. During the rainy season, it rains a lot! Last year (2010) was our first year here, and it was Guatemala's worst rainy season in 60 or 70 years! In fact, last year 318 bridges were either washed away or had so much damage they were unable to be used without repairs. But overall, we love the weather here!

19. Were you excited about moving?

The kids were really excited about moving, but they were kind of in shock and didn't know what to expect. When I asked the kids what they were excited about, they said:

1) Getting to go out of the country
2) Being a missionary
3) Meeting new people
4) Helping children

What were you nervous about:

1) Drinking the bad water
2) Speaking Spanish
3) They were sad about leaving their friends, but also excited about meeting new friends.

20. Do you go to the movies there?

We know of two movie theaters that show English movies. However, both of them are in the city, which is about forty-five minutes away. When we lived in the city, we would go sometimes, but since we moved in February 2011, we haven't gone. Now, we are bad Americans that buy bootleg DVDs off the side of the road for a buck or two. Don't tell the cops!

21. What American restaurants does Guatemala have?

We have McDonald's, Burger King, Domino's Pizza, Pizza Hut, Little Caesar's, Subway, Quizno's, Chucky Cheese, Tony Roma's, and they just opened an IHOP! Word is out that soon we'll have a DQ, Dairy Queen. The problem is most of these restaurants are in the city, which is about 45 minutes away. We only visit the city once or twice a month when we go to PriceSmart (which is like Sam's Club). But we now live close to Antigua which has many tourists from around the world, so even though there aren't a lot of American restaurants, there are a lot great places to eat. What is great about these places is that they are individually owned, so they are not a franchise. In fact, they are better than franchise which is awesome.

22. Is it more expensive or cheaper to live there?

Some things are cheaper; some are more expensive. Fruit and vegetables are much cheaper. Everything imported from the U.S. is much more expensive. Try paying $8 for a jar of peanut butter that you'd pay $3 for at Wal-Mart!

Gasoline and electricity are more expensive. We use more gasoline here because of the travel associated with being a missionary. Dave travels more than he did as a karate teacher in the States. However, even though electricity is more expensive, we use a lot less because the climate is mild enough that heat and A/C are not needed.

Renting a house is much less expensive here. Rent is a large portion of one's living budget and having a less expensive rent takes a lot of pressure off our budget. We were paying quite a bit more when we lived in Guatemala City (Mixco), which was for the first eight months we lived here, so this reduction in rent helps us breathe a lot easier.

All in all, the cost of living is cheaper here, except when you want stuff from the U.S. We are slowly using more, and eating more stuff made here; however, there is nothing like U.S. chocolate. The chocolate here is not good, and some foods that you just can't substitute!

23.   How do they celebrate the holidays?

The holidays are big here. They love fireworks. When it is someone's birthday, they will shoot off fireworks very early the morning of their birthday. Why, I do not know, but there are a lot of birthdays in Guatemala. They love to dance and listen to loud music. Their Independence Day is 15 September, and they have parties with loud music, food and fireworks, LOTS of fireworks.

Christmas is really big here. All the markets have many items for Christmas, much like you would buy in the U.S. They have lights, tinsel, ornaments, etc. The stores start selling Christmas items in August, if you can believe it. They don't have real Christmas trees here. They cut branches off of trees and staple them to a pole, but it looks very, very real. In fact Dave didn't realize this was done until after he bought the tree; that's how realistic the tree looks. They do not bake Christmas cookies like we do in the U.S. but make tamales. Everywhere you go people are selling tamales at Christmas time. Christmas Eve is their big celebration. They have a big dinner that night, and at midnight, everyone goes out, and they shoot off fireworks.

I mean tons and tons of fireworks, more fireworks than I have ever seen in my life. The fireworks go on and on for hours. And, they are not monitored like in the U.S.; anyone can shoot them off: kids, parents, teens, anyone. IT is crazy. Then they go inside and open all their presents, yup, at, like, 3:00 in the morning. They sleep late on

Christmas Day and just hang out. It is different. My kids love all the fireworks. You have to experience it to believe it. We have a video of it on the website.

Easter is another big holiday. They do not have Easter baskets and color eggs, or hide chocolate eggs like we do in the U.S. They have huge processions all depicting the crucifixion of Jesus Christ. They make huge murals of colored sand on the roads. It is amazing and takes them a long time to do.

24. What type of fruit and vegetables do they have?

Some of the fruits we don't have in the States are rambutans, which are fruits with a hard, fuzzy red exterior, and a soft interior that tastes something like a grape. We have fresh coconuts which they serve with a plastic straw for about $.60. When we drive to Antigua, we know where the coconut stand is, and we'll get fresh coconuts to drink. We also have apples, bananas, oranges, pineapples, and fresh mango. We have a lot of mango. We have papaya, but the kids really don't like it. Avocados are very common and inexpensive. We have tomatoes, cucumbers, spinach, and most of the typical vegetables that you have in the U.S. In fact, many of our fruits and vegetables are exported to the U.S

25.   How do you stay in touch with your friends?

Internet, Facebook, and Skype are so important. They have been lifesavers for us. It is wonderful to be able to keep in touch with friends and relatives this way. It is very difficult to get high speed internet where we live. It can be so frustrating to be talking to someone and get kicked off internet, but it happens very frequently (third world internet doesn't compare with high speed wireless internet). A rain storm can mess up our internet for a while. Sometimes the whole country just shuts down the internet. But, we are so thankful when it does work, and being able to stay in contact with those we love and miss so much.

26.   What were the biggest changes for you?

There were lots of changes. Things as simple as: not being able to drink tap water and everyone speaking Spanish was really difficult.   None of us spoke Spanish.   The language barrier was really bigger than we expected.

It was very difficult for Angie not being able to just hop in the car and drive to Wal-Mart or to the karate school or wherever. We were living in Mixco (Guatemala City), and it was dangerous, and we really didn't know where we were going; we didn't know our way around. So if Angie got lost, it wasn't like she could ask for directions. Also, we only had our 15 passenger van, and the driving in Guatemala City was really different than the States. No one follows traffic laws. They don't stay in their own lanes; they don't use blinkers; they drive really aggressive.

David loved it because it was more the style he liked for driving, but for Angie it became difficult because she was on lock down at our Condo and could only get out when either Dave was there, or when a friend could take her to the store.

When we actually went to the store, everything was different. They didn't have the same foods as the U.S., or if they did have the same foods, it definitely wasn't the same. Simple things such as milk, butter, ice cream, and chocolate didn't taste the same. When we found a U.S. brand, it was two or three times the cost!

In the U.S., going to Manna Church was a lot more than a couple of hours on a Sunday morning. Our church and our karate school was our life. Most of the Sgros would be found in about four places: our house, our karate school, Manna Church, or Taco Bell (Sam and Jesse loved hanging out with their friends at Taco Bell!).

Our karate school was located in a mall which had a movie theater, so the kids were always going to the movies. Safety wasn't even a concern. Everyone knew who they were. We knew all the security guards. We never thought about safety, as it wasn't a concern, but living in Guatemala City really changed everything. Imagine moving to a third world country, not speaking the language, not knowing the customs, not knowing culture, and then NOT KNOWING ANYONE. So, we moved to Guatemala not knowing anyone.

It really was a step of faith, a big step of faith! Many people told us they thought it was awesome what we were doing, but it really was a big step of faith. We knew it wasn't going to be easy. Of course other missionaries shared their experiences with us which let us be prepared for "something" to happen. So we knew it would be difficult; we just didn't know how difficult it was going to be!

27. Do kids really sell stuff on the road alone?

Yes, they do, from about five years old to old ladies. It is so sad to see kids selling flowers, gum, newspapers, toys, food, etc. When we ask where their mom is, they say "at home," surprised that we would ask. It is awful to see little old ladies and men begging on the streets, but it is a way of life for them.

28.   What is a fruit market?

Fruit markets are great, and we love going to them. This is where Mayan ladies sell all kinds of fruits and vegetables. Everything is out in the open, not at all like going to Wal-Mart or a grocery store in the states. You can bargain with them about the prices.   Families all work together. There are old women who have their daughters working at a stand nearby with their baby in their arms. You can buy the freshest fruits and vegetables here. They let you taste the fruit if you want. And, the fruit and vegetables are so much cheaper than the states. But, everything needs to be washed and soaked for about 20 minutes in a disinfectant before it is eaten. So, the prices are better, but it is a lot more work. I really like shopping at a market; the people are so friendly, and it is such a feeling of community.

29.   How do you renew your visas?

This is not fun at all. Every three months the visas have to be renewed. To do this, we have to leave the country which means a trip to Mexico. This is a five or six hour drive from where we live, and crossing the border is always an experience. The language barrier is tough; Mexico is hot, and there are not a lot of hotels that are nice enough to stay in. We have just applied for our temporary residency which will prevent us from having to leave the country every three months.

Thank God! Oh goodness, I thank God we don't have to go to Mexico every three months anymore! What a miserable time! Driving and trying to get into Mexico when everyone is telling you that you have to do "this" and you have to pay "that" and then it changes, so you don't have to do "this" or "that". They, the Guatemala side, was just try to get money from us! Thank you God; we are applying for our temporary residency.

30.   What was culture shock like?

It was tough, really tough. Everything was different. Different house, different food, different language, different stores, different stove, different people, different customs, different weather, different smells, different do's, different don'ts different, different, different, just different! Wow, was that ever difficult.

We were in a dangerous city; we couldn't go anywhere unless Dave was with us. Even when we went to a store, I didn't know where anything was or how to ask for it, and then I just couldn't find items I was used to cooking with. Everywhere we went there were Guatemalan people, of course, but it was so overwhelming, everyone speaking Spanish and so fast, and us unable to understand them. Church was filled with only Guatemalans; nothing was familiar about it.

Dave had to travel so much, and we had to stay home the whole time. I was used to going where I wanted when I wanted. It was quite an adjustment. It has been adjustments in areas we really never considered. Let me just say, I am so glad the first year is over.

31.   What is an example of a cultural difference that caused problems?

Time is perceived differently. For example, in the U.S. if we were going to meeting someone for breakfast at 8:30 A.M., it meant 8:30 A.M. Here it means 9:00 or 9:30 A.M. It's not uncommon for someone here to be 30 minutes to an hour late and not understand why you were upset. They'll show up 30 minutes to an hour late, laughing and smiling and not have a clue as to why you're upset, even if you had dinner ready and have been waiting all that time.

I asked someone, "If we said we were going to meet at 9:00 A.M., why would you show up 30 to 45 minutes late?" His answer brought great insight into the culture: "Why would I arrive at 9:00 A.M. when I know the other person wouldn't get there for another 30 to 45 minutes?"

Another thing is cake. I wasn't a big cake eater, but they love cake here in Guatemala. And, if you are offered cake, refusing it is a big offense, especially if it's a homemade cake. As I said, I am not a big cake guy. I don't really like sweets. But after offending a couple of folks, I was pulled aside, by a friend who explained that refusing cake would offend people. But I said, "I don't like cake!" He then said, "Say 'thank you,' and motion with your fingers that you'd only like a very small piece." So now I eat cake. I laugh when I am in the US and someone offers me cake and I smile and say "Yes", and motion with my fingers for a very small piece.

Here's another example I'm sure you can relate to: Let's say you walked into a store to buy a bed. And, let's say ALL the beds were either out of your price range, or more expensive then you wanted to pay. Here in the U.S. you'd say, "Thank you," and walk out. The salesman would say, "Have a good day," and it would be over....BUT not in Guatemala. The custom is: since you walked into their store for something, you need to walk out with something. So even though there was no chance I'd buy ANYTHING, the salesgirl took the time to write down the ID number for every bed we talked about.

She wrote down the model, and the price. I simply couldn't believe she was doing this, especially when I had no desire to buy and WANTED to leave. But I had to wait for her to finish. Then I had to be thankful that she took the time to do this for me. I forced a smile and left.

I soon realized that there was a big difference between living somewhere and visiting for a week. While I was frustrated that day, because I was in such a hurry, I've learned to slow down. I've learned that the process of buying and the interaction is just as important as the purchase. I understand now that when I reach an overseas call center, the first couple of minutes will be small talk about the weather and what not. I've also learned that it's rude to by-pass this short cultural dance. I've even come to enjoy it.

It slows things down and I think we, Americans, sometimes rush around and experience a lot of stress. What do you think? By the way, how's the weather? So, what did you do this weekend? Are you enjoying our book? Have you visited www.Godsroadtrip.com? Just so you know, the web site name is not case sensitive, but I don't like to write God with a little "g". And come to think of it, when I write about Him, I always capitalize the H, because He is simply awesome, and He is worthy. So, what's for dinner?

32.   Does Guatemala have American TV shows?

Yes, but it is different, For instance, "American Idol" is always shown a week later. We used to love to watch it together in the States, but it is a little frustrating to watch it a week later.   We already know who won; it's posted on Facebook. One of our favorites, "Biggest Loser", is not shown at all. We have to download it which takes a long time with our internet. But, they do have many other shows. We get The Disney Channel and Nick Jr. for the kids. All the Nick Jr. shows are in Spanish which is good for the kids. All commercials are in Spanish which is king of annoying sometimes. We are just glad that some of our favorites are shown here.

33.   How is are the churches there different?

The church we were going to in the city was very big. We were the only Americans there which drew attention to us and was quite an interesting experience. Also the music was so different from Manna's. Their music is very loud and jumpy. If you look around the church everyone is jumping up and down and yelling. I don't know how they can jump up and down for thirty minutes straight. Hahaha.

Recently after we moved to Sumango, we

found a small YWAN Church in Antigua which is strictly in English and is for American missionaries which really was a God send. It was really difficult to move here and attend a church which was so different. We really missed Manna Church. I think that was one of the most difficult aspects of being a missionary.

When we found the YWAM Church and was able to worship again in English and sing songs that we knew was like water to parched lips! Right now, we are praying and planning for opening our own church. The YWAM Church really was a blessing!

34.   What are the schools there like?

Well I feel like the schools are not as strict here. A lot of times, they have one teacher for thirty kids. Sometimes the teacher just doesn't show up to the class, so the kids just hang out. Also whenever we visit the schools, kids always come out and hang out with us, or they just stand by the door and do not pay attention to the class; the teachers don't do anything about it. I find it strange how all the kids skip class whenever they want or get up and leave the class and go to another class room. The teachers aren't very strict about having them pay attention.

35.   What are the houses like: poor, middle class, and rich?

The poor houses here have no, or little, electricity; the walls are cheap lamina (tin) or sometimes bamboo sticks, or corn stalk tied together They have dirt floor an open fire in the middle of the floor as their oven. They will have two beds for ten people. Normally, they only have two rooms, which are a kitchen and a bed room, and then they have an outhouse.

The middle class is how we live. We have electricity, running water, more than one bedroom, a living room, and a dining room. Middle class doesn't really lack anything.

The rich have nice, big houses. In many ways, it is similar to living in the U.S.; however, many may have a live-in maid and a chauffeur. We don't have a live-in maid and a chauffeur, but many families do.

36.   Are there malls in Guatemala?

They have really big, nice malls. Many of the malls here in Guatemala are better than the malls in the U.S. They sell a lot of American clothing and shoes. The malls are very Americanized, though the malls don't sell good ice cream like the States. Everything else is a lot like the States.

37.   Where do you go to school?

We home-school here, just like we did in the States.

38.   What kind of clothing do the Guatemalans wear?

There are traditional clothes that many of the Mayans wear: which is a very colorful shirt with a very colorful skirt which they hold up by a very colorful belt. There are many pictures on our website. However, there are people wearing American clothes, but you will see girls wearing Mayan clothing hanging out with girls wearing American clothes, so it doesn't matter what type of clothes you wear here.

39.   Are the people friendly?

Yes, the people are friendly; they try hard to make you feel welcomed here in Guatemala. They are always offering to help in any way they can.

40.   What is the medical care like?

You can get medical treatment here, and it's much cheaper than the states, though it's harder for us to explain "what's the matter." A lot of times, you don't have to make an appointment you can just show up, and they will see you. For instance, braces in the states cost $4,000.00-5,000, but here it cost close to $1,000.00.

You can get x-rays for about $30.00, and in the same day, they will read the x-ray and give you your results. A random visit to the doctors without insurance, including medicine, will be about $20.00. Liam had a slight concussion and had to go to the E.R. one night; the total cost for the CAT scan and the E.R. visit was around $150.00, and they apologized for it being so much. Also, three E.R. doctors were on call that night, and they spend probably two hours in our room with us talking while we waited for his results. The care is excellent here and much cheaper than the U.S. The language barrier can be frustrating, but they go out of their way to try and help us.

41.   Do they have heat and a/c?

No, most of the houses do not have either. You really don't need it. The poor just can't afford it even if it was available. Where we live, we use fans when we are hot and a fireplace when we are cold. The only place that I know of that has either heat and a/c is in the city in the very wealthy areas. You get used to this too and it saves on the electricity bill. Even though electricity is more expensive here, since we use much less electricity the over all bill is less.

42.   Do the houses have electricity?

Yes, most of the houses have some form of electricity. My house has normal amounts of electricity with plugs, and lights, outlets for a washer and dryer and stove. But, most of the extremely poor will have maybe one or two outlets, not many at all. They use wood to cook on, and hand-wash their laundry, and hang dry their clothes. They wouldn't even know how to use a washer or dryer.

43.   Do the houses have indoor bathrooms?

Yes, our house has an indoor bathroom and a lot of people have bathrooms much like in the states. But, again most of the extreme poor do not. They have terrible outdoor bathrooms with no running water. They do not have the ability to have a hot shower like we do. The public schools that we work in do have regular bathrooms, but they do not work and are just AWFUL.

44.   Do they have hot running water?

Well for us, we have a hot shower, and that is the only hot water in the house. But, most of the poor do not even have that, so I try hard not to complain; at least I have a hot shower. The device they use to give us hot water in the shower is called a widow maker, because it is just an electrified shower head. It sounds kind of strange; doesn't it, but you get used to it like so many other things here (see picture on the website).

45.   Can you drink the tap water?

No! We filter all our water. Whether it is for drinking or cooking, it all gets filtered. It is kind of strange not being able to drink out of the sink, but you get used to it. We make sure our short term Mission team members remember to brush their teeth with bottled water.   Chances are they wouldn't get sick from a little tap water, but why take the chance?

46.   Are there hotels, and what are they like?

Yes, there are hotels. It is like anywhere in the U.S.; some are very nice and some are not. In the city, they have hotels that have several swimming pools, spas, restaurants, stores, etc. in them. There are others that have no T.V., lumpy pillows, and just not somewhere you would want to stay with your family. Some hotels are really surprisingly nice!

47.   What are the most pressing issues you have noticed for women and girls?

I think one of the major issues for women and girls is that they are treated like second class citizens. They just are not valued very much. There is a lot of physical abuse, and in many homes, the father either leaves for another woman or to the U.S. never to return. In fact this is so common that when Dave was gone on one of his fundraising trips, a boy asked Natalie where her father was, and when she replied, "In the U.S.," he said, "Why? Does he not loves your mom anymore and has moved back there?" It's very sad, but it's something many kids deal with here.

As far as issues girls have to deal with, well, they have a great deal of work put on their shoulders at a very young age such as: caring for younger siblings, cooking, and housework. We see many girls as young as eight taking care of siblings all the time, carrying them around on their backs, and caring for them all day long. It is so sad that these girls do not get much of a childhood. We have a young girl that comes for Saturday breakfast every week. She is usually waiting at the door, with a baby strapped to her back, and two other siblings to care for. She is maybe twelve and has the sweetest smile. Their faces are always dirty, and when we serve lunch, they always have a third serving; it is so heartbreaking for me to see this. We always try to get her to stay afterwards for a craft, but she never does. She is one of the many children that keeps me awake and praying at night.

As in any country, the girls need to learn to value themselves and believe that they are special and created lovingly by a God who loves them and wants the best for them.

48. How do you do school being so busy?

Well, we just make school a priority even on busy days. We have a schedule and try really hard to stick to it. We consider being part of the ministry very important and part of their school. Practicing Spanish and helping the poor are all very important life lessons that cannot be learned from a book.

49. What has been the nicest experience you've gone through?

I think the nicest experience is how thankful the Guatemalans are for all the help we give them. The kids are always so thankful for the food and never complain about what we serve them. Often times the older kids will help us serve the kids after they have eaten. It is so neat to see Guatemalans helping other Guatemalans. Also, they would do almost anything to help us. I've had a teenage boy walk through the streets of Xenacoj at night helping me get out when the streets have closed down. They are very poor but so helpful and friendly, we could all learn a lot from them.

50. Do you call Guatemala home?

Yes, we feel like Guatemala is home. Of course, we still miss the American culture at times but every day we feel more and more at home here. Xenacoj is where our heart is now. We are praying to see if we, with some time, should buy land there. We'll see.

51. Will your children marry Guatemalans?

I think it is very possible that some of the children will marry a Guatemalan. Of course, that is all in God's hands, but we feel very comfortable here and believe that some of them will marry a Guatemalan. We love the people here and the kids have many friends both female and male.

52. What do you do for a doctor?

Well, we just recently found a great woman doctor right here in Xenacoj. She speaks only Spanish, but is very patient and somehow we can figure out what she means. In fact, she has said that if we have an emergency, she could come right to the house to see one of us. How helpful is that? When we first met her, we shared with her about us being missionaries, and we discovered she actually attends the church we use to attend in Guatemala City (Mixco). It's a small world even in Guatemala!

53. What is the saddest situation you've encountered?

I think that saddest thing to deal with is how poor and hungry the kids are. At a school where we work, they serve lunch for 1-3Q which is less than 50 cents. One day we were talking to a tiny girl and asked her if she was going to eat, but she said she could not afford the 3Q for a banana ($.36), and she had eaten nothing all day. We see many children who are in a similar situation. Things like that are so difficult and you just want to help them all.

One day there was a running race in town for the children. Some of our kids (the children that come to The Center) couldn't afford to pay the entrance fee. The fee was only 2Q per person ($.25), so these two little girls that come to the center were watching, and when I asked them if they were racing they said they had no money. We are talking about 50 cents here. So, we paid for them to race, and afterwards, they came up and gave me a huge hug. It was so sad that they couldn't join in, and I was so happy we could help them with such a little thing, and they were very thankful and appreciative.

We've really come to love these children and we really want to help them all. It's amazing that something as simple as food is a daily problem for them.

54. Why do you homeschool, and how long have you homeschooled?

We have homeschooled ever since my oldest who is now 21 was 5. We knew a family who was homeschooling and they started to talk to us about it, and it just seemed like the right thing to do. We home-school for many reasons: being able to pick and choose our own curriculum, working at the child's pace and not the pace some school board says is right, and being able to teach them about God and His amazing love. We did not want to be on some school's schedule but to create our own schedule, and now living in Guatemala, I am glad we did. The kids are able to help in the ministry a great deal because they can do what we do when we do it, not when they have time off from school. It has been a great experience for our family to home-school. Sometimes it is difficult, of course, but well worth the sacrifices.

55. Is it hard having a big family?

Sometimes it is hard having a big family. There is great responsibility. There are many personalities to deal with, fights, tears, lots of work, and laundry, but we would not change it for the world. We love having a big family and are so thankful that God has blessed us with one.

56. Would you adopt Guatemalan children?

Yes, if the opportunity ever came up, we would adopt some Guatemalan children. Our greatest desire is to help the Guatemalan people, and what better way to do that than to adopt some orphans and give them all the love, food, and help they deserve.

57. Do you have pets in Guatemala?

Yes, we have a little farm here. We have three German shepherds, four cats, with new kittens being born all the time, and two bunnies. Those are our pets; we also have farm animals. We have three pigs and 100 chickens. And by the time you are reading this, I'm sure the farm has expanded greatly! But for now, this keeps us very busy.

58. Have you met other missionaries in Guatemala?

Yes, we have met some other missionaries in Guatemala. There is a YWAM Church in Antigua, (thirty minutes from our house) and we have met other missionaries there. For a while we went to a Guatemala only church, which was difficult. So it is really nice to sing and worship in English, and it's nice to visit with other US Missionaries.

59. What is your favorite place in Guatemala?

We like a lot of places in Guatemala. Antigua is a beautiful city with many restaurants and beautiful views of mountains. Dave really loves it there. But, there are tons of tourists, so it can get kind of annoying with no privacy and just people everywhere.

We always love going to the beach, though. They are different than the beaches in the states, black sand and pretty dirty. But when we rent a beach house with a pool, it is great. We love the privacy and just being able to relax. But really, I would say Xenacoj is our favorite place. We feel like it is our village, and they are our people, and we love it there. There is a central park where the kids can play, a market where we can buy fruits and vegetables, and the kids play on the streets, and we just love it there. We consider this home now.

60. What is your weekly schedule like?

Sunday is our day of rest, and let me tell you we really need it. On Monday, we home-school all day. On Tuesday, we home-school in the morning and go to the center in the afternoon to teach karate and dance. On Wednesday, we school all day. On

Thursday, we home-school in the morning and go to the center in the afternoon to teach karate and dance. On Friday, we teach four hours of English at a public school and school in the afternoon. On Saturday, we cook eggs and serve food to the poor at the center, then karate and dance, then a movie in Spanish. It is a very busy schedule

61. Are the oldest kids (Rachel, Gabby, and Jesse) planning on staying in Guatemala?

They are still unsure of that. They love it here, but are not sure what God would have them do. There is college to consider and jobs in the states. It is all in God's hands.

62. Is the whole family in Guatemala involved in mission work?

Yes, the whole family is involved; it is great. Dave does all the fundraising, runs the mission trips, and basically makes sure everything runs smoothly. Angela makes and serves the food for the poor, and teaches English, and spends time with the kids. Rachel helps serve the food, and teaches English, and spends time with the kids. Gabby helps serve the food, teaches English and karate. Jesse helps with the food and has a break-dancing club at the center. Luke is our photographer. He does all the videoing and picture taking, and we really appreciate it. Olivia, Natalie, and Hope help serve the food, help teach English, karate and dance. Liam, Cole, and Vanni gather eggs daily and help clean them before we sell them. Noellia is loved by all the Guatemalans, sometimes too much. She does not like it when the girls touch her which they do all the time!

63. How do you live; how do you pay your bills; how do you make money?

Well, this is a challenge in a third world country. First, our home church is awesome! They support us every month. While it's not enough to live on, it is a big help. The second way a missionary receives money is through friends, family members, and fellow church members who believe in our work here in Guatemala and are a Ministry Partner. They'll pledge to send us "X" amount of dollars. This amount currently varies from $15 to $250 per month. Another way is some of my good friends and supporters will send funds when they have them. So, clear out of the blue a check will either come in the mail or through our Paypal account on www.goministries.info. (HINT! HINT! Lol, can't blame a missionary for trying!)

GO! Ministries, our non-profit corporation, give people a tax deduction for their donation. People like this, and being a legitimate U.S. non-profit corporation really speaks volumes to folks when they are considering supporting us.

Dave is a member of the CBBA, Christian Black Belt Association, and we are the official CBBA Missionary. The CBBA sponsors and partners with us on a monthly basis. Visit here to see the Christian Black Belt Association Website: (http://www.christianblackbeltassoc.org)

Before we moved to the mission field here in Guatemala, we owned a karate school. Dave taught karate full-time for 25 years and has always traveled a lot, teaching clinics and seminars. Dave has to travel to the U.S. a lot to do fundraising. He has many connections there and does a lot of martial arts seminars to help fund the ministry. It's a lot of work.

We have just recently discovered that we can sell eggs for extra funds here. Everyone eats eggs here; that is something that will never change, so we have 100 chickens. With some of the eggs, we feed the poor; the rest we are starting to sell. Both Jesse and Luke are a big help with this. The money buys the chicken food and the beans, Tampico (drink) and tortillas for our Saturday feeding program. Animals are very important for this area, so we are developing different plans to raise funds for the ministry with our animals. So, God always provides.

64. How does martial arts fit into your present and future?

Since several of our children are involved with martial arts, they do a lot of the teaching. Kids of any country want to do martial arts, and with as many friends as we have with karate schools, we have plenty of used uniforms and equipment to give away. In Guatemala it is relatively expensive to enroll in a karate school. Since we are teaching for free and give away the uniforms and equipment, there is no charge to the children. This lets many more children take class. Since 1985, we've always had a karate school, so teaching is natural.

Teaching karate helps build relationships and friendships. Having Tang Soo Do (karate) as a common bond, helps build a bridge. Often times this bridge becomes a way in which we share our faith.

Since the late 1970's, I, Dave, have been involved in competing in tournaments and now in hosting them, so our hope is to make a National Guatemala Competition Team and eventually enter the team into competition in the U.S.

Gabby has become the backbone of this school. As with my frequent travels, she is doing the majority of the teaching. She's doing a great job.

65. What are your plans for the future?

We have lots of plans for the future, but the most important thing is to make sure it is what God wants us to do. We would like to start a feeding program for the public school that we work with. Most of the kids do not get breakfast, so we want to get enough chickens that we would have enough eggs to feed them daily. There are 530 children in that school so that is a lot of eggs. We have an idea for opening an orphanage; there are many orphans in Xenacoj. We need to listen to the voice of God and find out what He wants us to do.

We also would like to apply for permission to run an orphanage. Our thoughts are that it would be best (at this time) to hire "House Mothers" to raise the children. We, the missionaries, would make sure they have what they need, over see the orphanage, and be there as a support system.

We've received more interest for more short term mission teams to visit, and our faith is really growing, so by the time you read this, I can't say where we will be!

66. What are the difficulties in reaching a people who are so poor and have a different culture, language, and religion?

Well, the first major difficulty is language! The older folks in Santo Domingo Xenacoj speak *Caqchikel* which is one of the 23 different Mayan languages spoken here in Guatemala (not dialects, but different languages!) So, it is very difficult to communicate with the older folks who do not speak Spanish.

With folks being very poor, there is a very different mindset. Many of their day to day problems can be solved for less than $10. However, if all we do is pay to solve people's problems, we will quickly have a ministry that serves as an ATM to solve problems.

The long term solution is to help equip the Mayans to solve their own problems. This is a challenge because we U.S. Americans are goal setters and getters. We have vision and are time oriented. We measure our steps and adjust our daily actions based on the results. This is VERY different from the mindset we are living amongst.

Most Mayans don't really think about tomorrow or setting goals, or evaluating their progress. To paraphrase Proverbs 29:18, "Where there is no vision the people perish." So for us to help the Mayans long term, we will need to teach some business and planning concepts. It will take time, and it must be done in a way that fits into their world, so we cannot just transplant our mindset into Guatemala. That will cause other problems that we can't even begin to imagine at this time.

67. What is the foundation of your work there?

We want to live for Christ and not for ourselves. We want to show God's love to people. We do this by loving them. The people we are serving are considered second class citizens here. Many other Guatemalans don't really speak to the Mayans. Many Mayans work as servants for the upper classes. Most Guatemalans wouldn't hug or kiss a Mayan, but we do both. A typical Guatemalan family would never consider marrying a Mayan, but for us, people are people, and we love the Mayans. We want our children to marry the one person God has for them, Mayan or not.

I know for a fact that this particular statement would be very difficult for many Guatemalans to accept and comprehend. This is cultural, and as U.S. Americans, we too have our cultural beliefs that others would not understand.

We want to show the Mayans the love of Christ. We try to do this in many ways. One way we do this is by feeding them; we try to help people get medicine and clothing. When teams visit they play with the children. The foundation of our work is to try to be the hands and feet of Jesus, and to teach our children to likewise.

68. Do you ever feel discouraged or disappointed in events that occur?

Heck yeah! Living in another country is not easy by any means! Even after being here for a year, it's still very hard to communicate. Dave has to travel back to the U.S. a lot, and it's not easy having our family separated. The culture is very different here, and we're THE FOREIGNERS, so we have to learn to adjust.

Sometimes the laid back, slower pace drives Dave crazy: knowing he'd have "this" done hours ago in the U.S. and then he has to remind himself that it's in God's hands, not ours. Being a missionary is as rewarding as it is difficult, but we wouldn't change anything, and we have no regrets about being here and serving here.

69. In living by faith, how have you seen God's faithfulness show up in incredible ways?

We see Gods hand all the time. I joke that, for me, living in Guatemala is like the cartoon where the guy is sleep walking, and when he steps off the roof, a metal beam catches him, and when that ends, there is another beam, and this continues until he reaches the ground.

Let me give you a simple, typical example:
The other day I took our dog to the vet. He was very sick. My Spanish wasn't strong enough to answer the vet's questions, so I went to call a friend to translate. Almost every time I call him on the phone, I can talk with him, but today I caught his answering machine. So I called another friend, but she was busy and couldn't talk. This went on with every person that could usually help me. I stepped outside to make another call (because it was getting loud in the store) and a woman, in perfect English, says, "Is that puppy called a German Shepherd?" She translated for me.

But the part I wanted to share with you is that she usually isn't in this part of the market. The vet is also her pastor, and she felt the Hoy Spirit lead her to his store today because she felt he would need help! It turns out she is an English teacher and will help us in our church.

70. Does each of you have a Bible verse that speaks to you personally?

For me, Dave, Matthew 25:34-40 really speaks to me: vs. **34** "Then the King will say to those on his right, 'Come, you who are blessed by my Father; take your inheritance, the kingdom prepared for you since the creation of the world. **35** For I was hungry and you gave me something to eat, I was thirsty and you gave me something to drink, I was a stranger and you invited me in, **36** I needed clothes and you clothed me, I was sick and you looked after me, I was in prison and you came to visit me.'

37 "Then the righteous will answer him, 'Lord, when did we see you hungry and feed you, or thirsty and give you something to drink? **38** When did we see you a stranger and invite you in or needing clothes and clothe you? **39** When did we see you sick or in prison and go to visit you?'

40 "The King will reply, 'Truly I tell you, whatever you did for one of the least of these brothers and sisters of mine, you did for me.'

This portion of scripture has really meant a lot to me.

71. Does each of you have a personality in the Bible that you relate to?

I don't really have one person. Sometimes when Peter does bone-head things, I have to laugh because it reminds me of things I've done. Paul can really rub people the wrong way, and I can definitely relate to that. John is just way too nice, and at times that gets on my nerves. I'm just being honest. Thomas is a bit depressing; I'm more positive than that. I like Peter's and Paul's mentality. Once I set my mind on doing something, I usually do it, and the harder it is to do it, the more determined I am to get it done. Don't tell me what I can't do.

72. Are you guys willing to have more kids of your own?

We would love to have more children. That is all in God's hands, but we would welcome a baby with much happiness. Please pray that the Lord with bless us with a child (or three) more!

73. What role has prayer played in the decisions that you have made?

Prayer is like the heat and a/c in my house when we lived in Fayetteville, NC. It was always on and set the atmosphere in the room. When we lived in Fayetteville, I used to go to Sammy Choi's Thursday 5:30 - 6:30am prayer meeting. I miss that a lot.

Praying and having pray partners is like oxygen. I don't know how one can call themselves a Christian and not have an intense prayer life. We pray a lot. The Bible says to "pray without ceasing". That's a lot of praying! So we pray a lot. We have really grown in or faith, and in depending on God. And if you think about it, isn't that the way it's supposed to be anyway? Lord, forgive my unbelief!

74. How has living in Guatemala changed your family dynamic?

For one thing, we are together all the time. In the U.S., everyone had their own things that they did. This one went to dance, this one to karate, this one had a job, etc. but here when we go out, we go out together. We all work in Xenacoj together. It really has been great. I really love that we are able to do this together.

75. Where do you buy clothes?

They have malls here, of course, but they are expensive. We have discovered this huge thrift store here called, Mega Paca, and we do most of our shopping there. They have tons of clothes and shoes at great prices. They have lots of American brands that they get from the states, so we have found some great clothes there at really great prices.

76. What has been an impactful miracle that the Lord has done?

Seeing hundreds of children come to the Lord through our family ministry really makes me smile.

77. Do you work with a church in Guatemala?

When we lived in Mixco (Guatemala City) we worked with a Church for the first eight months.

Now that we've opened a church, our plate is pretty full, but I can definitely see us continuing to work from time to time with other churches, absolutely.

78. What spiritual warfare have you encountered?

Every time Dave leaves Guatemala, we feel the attacks of the enemy. One time the electricity got shut off, even though he had just paid the bill a few days before. This was a real problem because things are done differently here, and this was the first time we had to deal with this. So it was a challenge just to figure out why it happened. Then we had to figure out how to resolve it. All this had to be done through translators, over phones. It took quite bit of effort and time. Everything takes longer here in Guatemala.

We've had kids get sick and had to figure out how to get to the doctor's at 9:00 P.M. on a Friday night. This last time the week he was leaving, the brakes on the van went out, the motor on the window broke, and I was so sick, I was in bed for two days. Right before mission trips all of a sudden someone will get sick, or something will break, etc. etc. It is crazy, and we do feel it a lot. We just try to remind ourselves that this is all part of it, and it is because we are doing great things for the Kingdom of God that we know the enemy wants to foil our plans. In fact, we've come to the place that every time Dave gets ready to leave, we joke about it. We expect it, and knowing that the enemy will attack, when we see it, we recognize it.

Since I, David, know spiritual warfare happens every time we host a team, make plans to fundraise, or be separated from the family, I've really felt my awareness go up as to what's natural and what's Spiritual warfare. And I have to be honest, there are times I think, "Wow, that ol' devil is pretty crafty." He never ceases to amaze me with how he attacks us, BUT, (Imagine sitting in a chair watching a movie) it's like watching a movie on the screen; the devil attacks, and then the Lord does His thing, and if you hang in there enough you'll see the Lord's thing is bigger and better then the devil's thing.

I have to laugh, sometimes when I feel under attack; I just read this scripture:
Revelation 20:10 NIV

"And the devil, who deceived them, was thrown into the lake of burning sulfur, where the beast and the false prophet had been thrown. They will be tormented day and night forever and ever."

So when he gives me grief, I just quote this and laugh...have a nice day devil. And it's not just me, but we (as a family) are growing spiritually and learning more and more to hear the voice of God, so we are beginning to recognize earlier when we are dealing with spiritual warfare. Because of this we have grown in our prayer life. Because prayers are all based on faith, the enemy really hates unity and prayer. But the Bible says it's impossible to please God without faith, so we pray a lot, and it really helps!

79. Have any of you gotten sick down there?

Yes! Once, the kids all had parasites one time. That was awful. The doctor said it is very common here and it could have come from anything they ate but probably fruit that wasn't clean. We went to a public hospital for care which was free and were treated great. We've had teeth pulled, infections, slight concussions, and minor problems. We were treated great everywhere we went, and the healthcare is really cheap. Liam had a CAT scan and we've cleared the "what if" medical concern. Many people ask us this, and we have seen the results, first hand!

80. What are the main problems that you see in Guatemala?

There is a lot of poverty which leads to a lot of crime. There is a lot of political corruption which leads to social instability and mistrust. Guatemala is part of the drug highway between South America and the U.S.A. which again means violence and gangs.

There are many orphans. Schools don't have adequate funding. All these lead to problems especially for the single mothers and the orphaned children. I think this is why my family is here serving the Mayans. We really love serving in Xenacoj.

81. How do you know you stand out in Guatemala?

In Xenacoj where we work, there are no other Americans working here on a regular basis. We know we stand out because we get stared at all the time. Some of them just have never see Americans except on television. Also, some people will see us and beg for money because we are Americans, so we must be rich. Again they only know what they have seen on T.V. The girls are quite popular with the boys here. One thing we have noticed here is that the boys are a lot more aggressive than in the U.S., and they don't take "no" for an answer very well. But they are learning quickly that Dave, Dad, is watching!

82. How often do you come back to the U.S.?

The family has not been back since we moved here in June of 2010. Dave travels back quite a lot. Jesse and Gabby both were able to go back with him on one of his visits for a trip. They got to reconnect with their friends, and that was nice for them. We plan on going back in February of 2012.

83. Is there a final story you'd like to share?

The kids we love at Xenacoj showed us how they love us yesterday, August 2011. My sister Rachel lets the kids use her phone to play games and such. One boy was using it, and we were all playing around. When Rachel asks for her phone, we realize the boy has stolen the phone and ran off.

A lot of the kids say they are sure who they saw take it and tell us they are going to go look for him. They ran off looking for him while the other kids were helping us look for it. When they came back saying they couldn't find it, a boy offered to take us to the boy's house. So we started going to his house when Rachel and I realize that we have a ton of kids around us offering their help and trying to find the phone.

My dad came with us and told us to count how many kids there are. We counted 30 kids! I can't believe it! We are only looking for a phone, and yet we have 30 kids around us helping us look for it running here and there trying to find out where he is and where he lives. Finally someone sees him and runs after him and grabs him saying he found the boy.

My dad asks where the phone is, and he says

more than once he doesn't have it, and he didn't steal it. He blames it on a six year old boy who was with us the entire time. So we knew he wasn't telling the truth. Finally he admits that he stole it and was going to sell it to his friend. So we go to his house, and he gets his phone. During this whole time all 30 kids follow us around helping in every way they can. I still can't believe everything they did to get a phone back.

84. **How can we help you, your family, and your ministry?**

1) First and foremost, we need prayer. Please pray for us. We face many challenges living in a 3rd World Country. We face difficulties in the language; customs, and the cultural differences between not just the US and Guatemala, but also here between the Mayans and the Guatemalans. So, we face two different cultures here in Guatemala. We're still learning our way around, in every sense of the word. While we're pass the "Honeymoon Phase", we're still very new missionaries. So please pray for us.

2) I know this sounds simple, but please don't forget us! We're a long way from home. We're a long way from friends and family. We miss what we use to know. Life is very different for us now. It is exciting, but at time it is still very hard. I can't expect you to imagine how refreshing it is to get a quick unexpected 'Hey,

how's it going?" e-mail from a friend. We love being missionaries, but there are times it is tough, really tough, and hearing from old friends can really be encouraging, especially when it seems like we are in the cross-hairs of the enemy!

3) Partner with us. We live on faith, which means our only financial support comes from you! Seriously, we are able to live and work in the mission field because of support that comes from our friends, both individuals, Churches and Karate Schools alike. If you believe in the work we're doing here then join "Team Guatemala" and send either support on a monthly basis or as funds allow.

In the 18 months we've been on the mission field we've seen several missionaries pack up their things and their families and move back home because their funding dried up. What does this mean? Well, you'd be surprised by how few people actually support us on a regular monthly basis. Ask yourself this: "Do we believe in the work the Sgro family is doing in Guatemala?" If you answered "yes"to us, could we support GO! Ministries (A 501 (c) (3) non-profit corp) with a monthly tax-deductible donation of $20, $25, $50, $100? If you are not partnering with us on a monthly basis is it something you would consider doing? To do so you can send a monthly check made out to "GO! Ministries"

Send to:
GO! Ministries
PO Box 393
Pittsford, VT 05763

Dave is flying back and forth to the US to raise support, and because of his friendships and relationships with his students he will always continue to visit them in the US. But being a missionary is all based on living on faith and we constantly need to fundraise. Adding a faithful regular supporter provides much more than financial support, it provides stability in an uncertain world! So we covet your prayers and thank you for continued monthly financial support and your priceless friendship!

85. What are you plans for the next "Chapter" or next year couple of years?

This is our first book. It is a lot of work! But it also was a lot of fun. Having everyone work together and sharing ideas and information was an interesting project. Also, as we home school, it was a great English project. Life is meant to be lived, and for the Sgro family, life is meant to be lived to bring glory to God! The subject matter for this book ended around the end of July 2011. The final editing of this book is the end of October. Because of this much has already happened in the last three months. As I am writing this, we're looking for a house to rent living in Santo Domingo Xenacoj. Right now we live four miles away and drive in. I'm sure our life will drastically change when we move into Xenacoj.

We currently have 100 chickens. We'd like to expand our chicken farm. We'd like to expand our feeding program. In February 2012 our entire family is coming back to the U.S.A. for the first time since we moved to Guatemala. I can't wait to see how their perceptions of the U.S.A. have changed! It will also be interesting to see how our family reacts when we return to Guatemala after our first visit back to the States. It's all so new! We're really coming around the block for the first time. We do know that we see God's hand a lot. We do know we've grown spiritually quite a bit. We do know it really is different living outside the U.S. especially in an extremely poor and violent country like Guatemala. But, we also know "Life is an adventure, so live it!"

"The day the Americans came to town"

Our first book "Living the Dream" was about how our family of 15 went from living in the suburbs of Fayetteville, NC to moving and working amongst the Maya (one of the 23 different Indigenous people of Guatemala).

Our second book, "The day the Americans came to town", is about our family living in Xenacoj amongst the Maya people. Without a "bathroom", but rather a toilet closet that opens to the common room, water available every other day, and one large gray concrete water tank. in which we shave, brush our teeth, wash dishes and clothes (by hand) from the one large gray concrete water tank, it would be safe to think our friends in the US would say we lack much.

But to our neighbors we're the "Rich Gringos" (Americans) that live in town. With a car, a 15 pass van (Team Bus) a hot shower, many appliances, a modern stove, (not an open fire), each child with their own bed, "The day the Americans came to town" will provide you with insight into the challenges and rewards of our family has come to realize we are, in fact, very rich, and that we live amongst a people with a rich past (They Mayans were once one of the powerful peoples in Central America) and a wearisome; archaic toilsome future.

Read how we walk a balance between the extreme religious where a rash on one of our children is considered a "plague", (because we didn't pray enough), and the extreme superstitious where the neighborhood children talk about witches walking through walls and mythical animals (a cross between a dog and a horse) that live on the edge of the city, (where the concrete ends and the forest begins). They've never seen them, but their parents and Uncles have.

One foot is in the ancient past and the other is in the modern future with wifi, cell phones, and cable TV.   Look for book number 2: "The day the Americans came to town", due out in early 2012.

In Closing

In closing we would really like to thank Senior Pastor Michael Fletcher. He is a visionary and always amazes me with his insight. We'd like to thank Pastor Tommy Cartwright. He's been a tremendous help and is always more than willing to take my phone calls, of which there have been a countless amount. We'd also like to thank Pastor Michael Pacella. He saw and believed in me as a Minister long before I ever saw and believed in it for myself.

I'd like to thank Cindy Barrington and Aubrey Sgro for editing this book, especially on such short notice! We'd also like to thank our Board of Directors; Jim and Pam Bierman, Pastor Michael Pacella, and Erin Martin - you guys rock! We at GO! Ministries have the best Board of Directors! They have been very patient, and supportive. I know they pray for us all the time and always offer an encouraging word. When we were going through some very dark times here in Guatemala, they were a burst of light! So thanks; thanks a lot.

I, David, want to thank Angela (my most amazing wife) and my thirteen awesome children, Aubrey, Sam, Rachel, Gabby, Jesse, Luke, Olivia, Natalie, Hope, Liam, Cole, Cole, COLE? (Inside joke), Giovanni and Noellia! GO! Ministries (and certainly I) would not be where we are without

Angela. She really is the backbone of it all and even these words fail to truly express and pale in comparison to my true feelings.

Lastly, I want to thank my Lord and Savior Jesus Christ. You are so awesome, so wonderful, so amazing, so everything! I'll never know how much it cost to see my sin up on that cross. Lord, I'll never even begin to comprehend how and why you love us like you do, but I sure am glad you do!

GO! and make disciples!

Together Changing Guatemala!
Love, The Sgro Family

www.ingramcontent.com/pod-product-compliance
Lightning Source LLC
Chambersburg PA
CBHW060528030426
42337CB00034B/2170